Peekaboo!

It's Mommy!

Who's playing behind the toys?

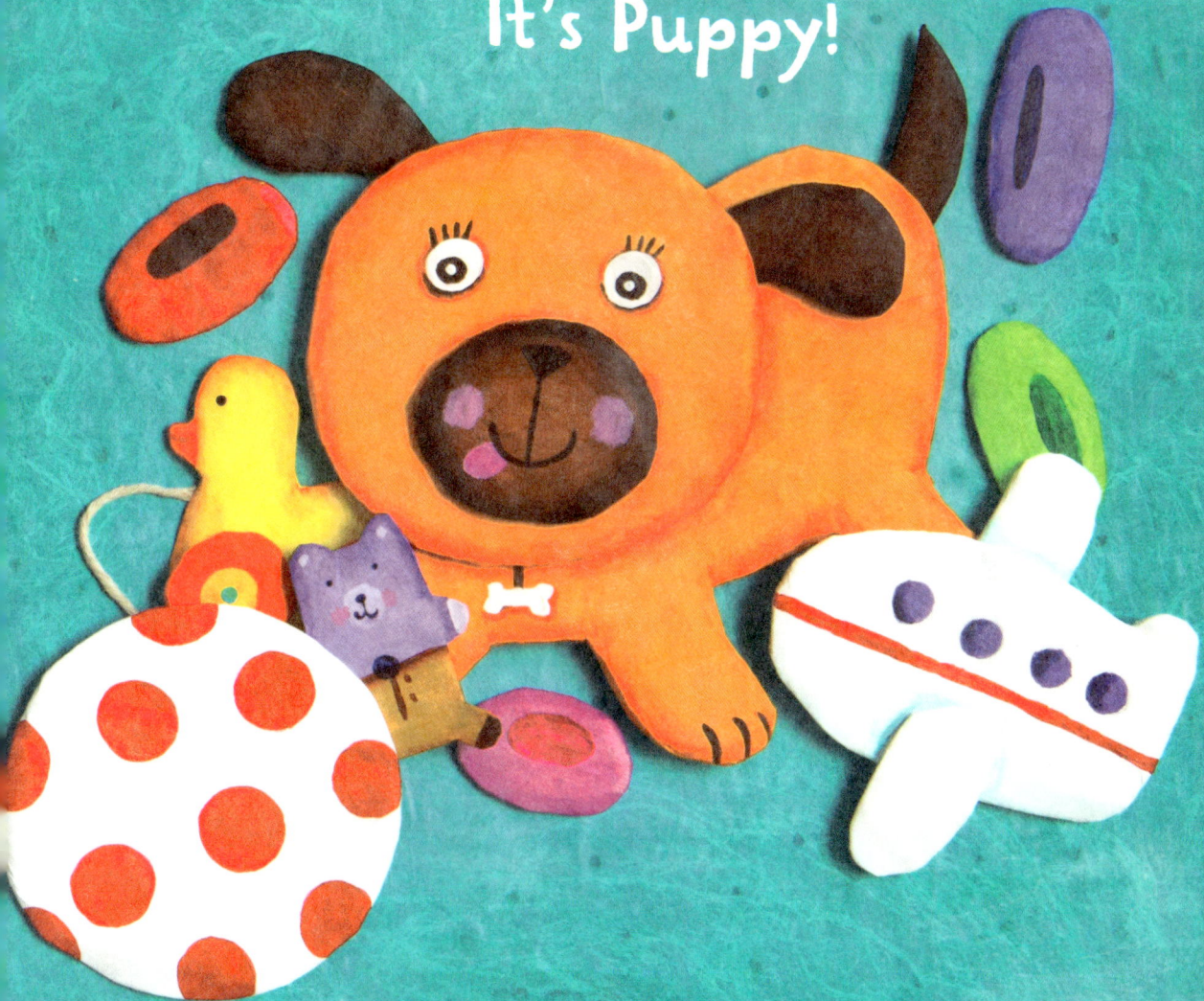

Peekaboo!
It's Puppy!

Who's that reading a book?

Peekaboo! It's Daddy!

Who's hiding behind the yarn?

Peekaboo!
It's Kitty!

Who could that be under the covers?

Peekaboo! It's ME!

BOOKS BABIES CAN REALLY SINK THEIR GUMS INTO!

Who's hiding behind the curtains? It's Mommy!
Who's playing behind the toys? It's Puppy!
Who's hiding under the covers? It's Baby!

Play peekaboo with Baby
in a book that's INDESTRUCTIBLE.

Dear Parents: INDESTRUCTIBLES are built for the way babies "read": with their hands and mouths. INDESTRUCTIBLES won't rip or tear and are 100% washable. They're made for baby to hold, grab, chew, pull, and bend.

LOVE YOU BABY

RHYME WITH ME!

THIS LITTLE PIGGY

BABY, LET'S COUNT!

HOME SWEET HOME

← CHEW ALL THESE AND MORE!

THE ITSY BITSY SPIDER

HELLO, FARM!

THINGS THAT GO!

BABY, FIND THE SHAPES!

BABY, LET'S EAT!

$5.95 US   ISBN 978-0-7611-8181-1

5 0 5 9 5

9 780761 181811

All INDESTRUCTIBLES books have been safety-tested and meet or exceed ASTM-F963 and CPSIA guidelines. INDESTRUCTIBLES is a registered trademark of Indestructibles, LLC.
Contact specialmarkets@workman.com regarding special discounts for bulk purchases.
Printed by Druk – Intro S.A., Poland